Volleyball

R U L E S

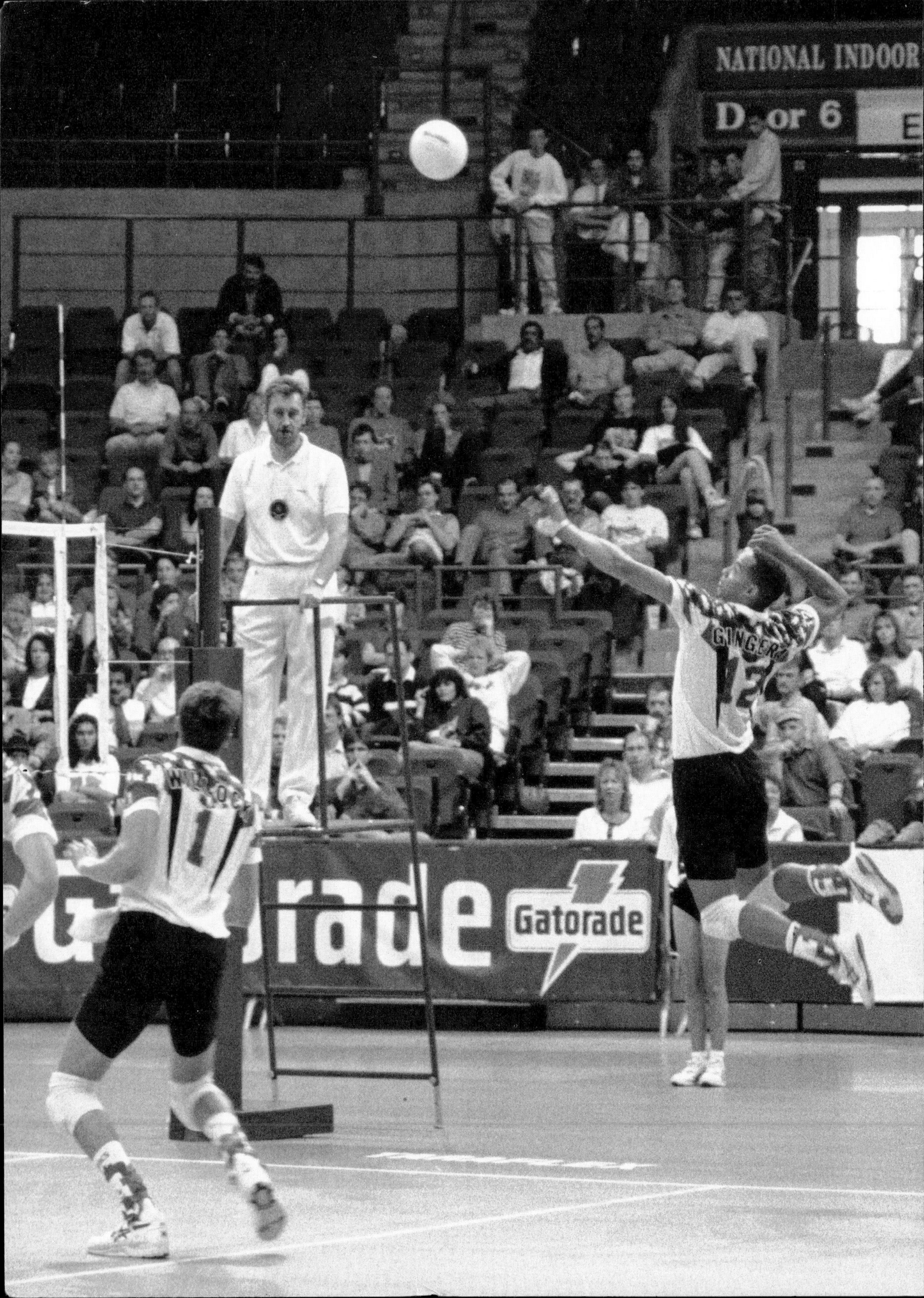
NATIONAL INDOOR
Door 6
GINGER
12
1
Gatorade

Volleyball

R U L E S

BERNARD KILKENNY

WARD LOCK

A WARD LOCK BOOK

First published in the UK 1997
by Ward Lock
Wellington House, 125 Strand
LONDON WC2R 0BB

A Cassell Imprint

Distributed in the United States
by Sterling Publishing Co., Inc.
387 Park Avenue South, New York,
NY 10016-8810

A British Library Cataloguing in Publication
Data block for this book may be obtained from
the British Library

Photographs by B.M. Totterdell

ISBN 0 7063 7525 4

Typeset by Business Color Print, Welshpool,
Powys, Wales

Printed and bound in Great Britain by
The Bath Press

Frontispiece Dynamic play from Canada's
Randy Gingera, as the referee Jeff Brehaut
looks on.

CONTENTS

INTRODUCTION

Volleyball is arguably one of the world's top three participation sports; it has an estimated 250 million players worldwide and 210 different countries are affiliated to the International Volleyball Federation, more than are affiliated to a world governing body for any other sport – including football!

In essence volleyball is a simple game which can be played by anyone, at any level; its worldwide popularity stems from the fact that it can be played almost anywhere – inside a sports hall or gymnasium, or outside on grass or sand. All that is needed for a friendly game is a ball and a net or rope to knock the ball over. Played at its best, volleyball is one of the most exciting and spectacular sports in the world.

Volleyball is a team sport played by both men and women, in which the rules for men and women are essentially the same. There are internationally recognized versions of the game for introducing the sport to very young players (mini volleyball) and for players with physical disabilities (standing/sitting volleyball). The indoor (six-a-side) version has been an Olympic sport since the Tokyo Games of 1964; it has now been joined by the two-a-side beach game (played on sand) which made its successful Olympic debut at Atlanta in 1996. It is possible to play mixed volleyball and with all the other informal varieties – recreational volleyball, trimvolley (a fitness version of the game, played mainly in Scandinavia), family volleyball, all the beach variations and a nine-a-side game which developed independently in Asian countries – volleyball is truly a sport for all.

Volleyball is distinguished from other sports by three essential features; first, it is a team game in every sense of the word. Although there is increasing specialization of roles at the higher levels of play, the concept of 'rotation' ensures that all players must learn to play in every position around the court. The rules also specify the need to pass the ball between players, as opposed to being able to retain personal possession within a team; they also limit the number of passes allowed between team members before the ball must be sent to the opponents. A weaker player cannot effectively be hidden and, conversely, a strong player cannot win the game alone.

Second, volleyball has precise rules that determine the exact manner in which the ball can be touched; even a winning shot can be overruled, if the ball contact is made using an incorrect technique. Although recent rule changes have tended to reduce the traditional importance of using perfect control when playing the ball, the concept of 'handling' remains one of volleyball's distinguishing characteristics and continues to be a great source of debate (and argument) among the game's players, coaches and referees.

Finally, volleyball is a non-timed, non-contact sport which is controlled by strict rules on behaviour and discipline – for example, only the captain may speak to the match officials during a game. Other aspects of match protocol and team etiquette – the warm-up, the toss, the team line-up, the bench personnel, the procedures for substitutions and time-outs and the sanctions awarded for misconduct or delaying the game – are laid down in the rules. This ensures

that a volleyball match, whether played by professionals or amateurs, is governed according to an agreed code of conduct where the match officials will intervene only rarely, in order to ensure that the game is played according to the spirit of the rules.

Volleyball's simplicity as a ball game for players of all standards, its technical appeal as a non-contact sport requiring passing skills and teamwork, the many different forms in which it can be played and its universal nature as a sport for anyone who wishes to enjoy a competitive, athletic pastime which is played to a fair and sporting code of conduct, all make it a great game to play.

The aim of this book is to explain the rules to those who are just beginning to realize how good volleyball is – the parents of young players who may be taking the sport at school, teachers who may not have had a formal introduction to refereeing, students needing a broad outline of the rules, and all those players and coaches of the game who may not wish to qualify as referees but for whom a good basic understanding of the rules can assist greatly in getting the best out of their play and the most out of their team.

All of the main references in this book relate to the Official Rules as agreed by the Fédération Internationale de Volley Ball (FIVB), the world governing body for the sport; unless indicated otherwise, the rules relate to the indoor six-a-side game.

The author, as President of the Referee Commission for the English Volleyball Association, is also responsible for rules interpretations and all other officiating matters in this country. Whilst this book has the official authorization of the English Volleyball Association, any views expressed within are those of the author alone.

● AUTHOR'S NOTE

Volleyball is a game played by both men and women; where references are made in this book to 'player', 'coach' or 'referee', these terms are taken to apply equally to male and female.

● ACKNOWLEDGE-MENTS

The author wishes to thank Steve Walton and Jeff Brehaut for work done on the Sitting Volleyball and Beach Volleyball sections respectively. Thanks are also due to Keith Nicholls, Barbara Totterdell and Sam Sweetman for helpful suggestions made during proof-reading.

● CONVERSION TABLE

Approximate conversion table for countries using non-standard (imperial) measurements

2cm	=	0.79in
5cm	=	2in
10cm	=	4in
65cm	=	25.6in
67cm	=	26.4in
80cm	=	31.5in
1m	=	3ft 3in
1.8m	=	5ft 11in
2.24m	=	7ft 4¼in
2.43m	=	7ft 11⅜in
3m	=	9ft 10in
7m	=	23ft
9m	=	29ft 6in
9.50m	=	32ft
18m	=	59ft
260g	=	9oz
280g	=	10oz
0.30kg/cm²	=	3.5lbs/sq in
0.325kg/cm²	=	4lbs/sq in
10° Celsius	=	50° Fahrenheit

GAME
CHARACTERISTICS

Volleyball is played on a court which is divided by a high net; the object of the game is for the players on one side to hit the ball over the net and make it land on the opponents' court. The ball is served into play by a back-court player, who stands off court and hits the ball over the net. At this precise moment, all of the players must be standing in specific positions, but as soon as the rally begins they may move around anywhere on their own side of the net. Each team is allowed three touches to stop the ball landing on court and to return it to the other side. The rally continues until the ball touches the ground, goes 'out' or until some other playing fault is committed by one of the players. Although the ball may contact any part of the body, it is usually played in one of four main ways: with the forearms (the basic defensive play, usually referred to as the 'dig'), with the fingers (usually in the form of the 'volley' pass that gives the sport its name) and with the open hand (as in the service and the attack-hit) or with the hands (as when blocking the ball at the net).

Except in the final set, only the serving team can score a point. When the serving team wins a rally it scores a point and continues to serve; when the non-serving team wins the rally it gains the right to serve next and its players must rotate one position clockwise around the court. A set is won by the first team to score 15 points, providing it has a two-point lead. The match is won by the first team to win three sets.

With the entry of beach volleyball into the Atlanta Olympics of 1996, volleyball can no longer be considered to be a single game; it is now a family of games. The standard rules described here may increasingly be modified and adapted to represent the variety of different versions being played the world over, and to reflect the true universality of volleyball as a sport for everyone.

FACILITIES AND EQUIPMENT

● THE PLAYING AREA

The **playing area** for volleyball is made up of the actual **playing court**, a rectangle measuring 18m × 9m, and the **free zone**, a symmetrical area surrounding the court measuring at least 3m wide all round. The playing area must be free from all obstructions to a height of at least 7m above the floor.

The **playing surface** – normally wooden or synthetic – must be flat, horizontal and uniform throughout its whole area; it should not be rough or slippery and must not present any danger of injury to the players (who may fall onto, or dive across, the floor during play). The lines that mark out different areas on the court are all 5cm wide and should be either painted or taped. Such lines are considered to be part of the area they mark out: hence, for example, a ball which lands on a line is considered to be in.

A **centre line,** directly below the net, divides the court into two halves. The lines surrounding the court are called the **side lines** and the **end lines.** An **attack-line** is marked in each half of the court, parallel to the centre line and 3m from it; this line divides each court into a **front zone** and a **back zone.** The front zone is considered to extend into the off-court area; players who should be in the back zone are prevented from making certain types of play in this region.

The **service zone** is a 9m wide area at each end of the court; it extends as far back as the available free zone allows. The **substitution zone** is the area near the scorer's table in which all player substitutions must be made. It is bounded by the imaginary extension of the two attack-lines.

In the corner nearest each team bench, outside the free zone, is a **warm-up area** for the substitutes.

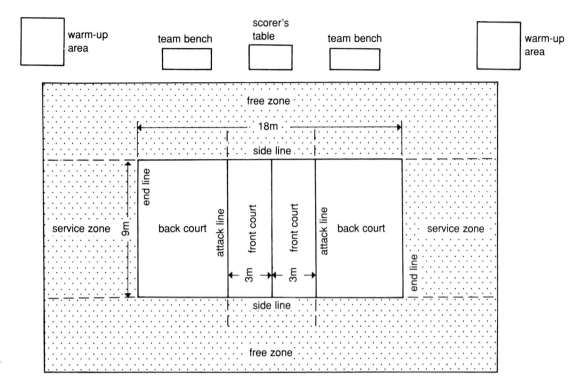

The minimum temperature for a volleyball sports hall is 10°C.

The playing area consists of the playing court plus the rectangular free zone around it. The size of the free zone (which includes the service zone) varies according to the level of competition.

● THE NET

The **net** is 9.50m long and 1m deep; it must be tensioned correctly and hung directly over the centre line. The net should be black and made of 10cm square mesh. At the top of the net is a white band and down each side, directly over each side line, is a white **vertical side band.** Fastened immediately outside the side bands are two **antennae** – flexible rods

usually made of fibreglass, measuring 1.80m long; the ball may not touch the antennae during play and they effectively mark out the area where the ball must cross over the net during a rally.

The official height of the net for men is **2.43m**, measured at its centre; the height for women is **2.24m**. The two ends of the net, measured over the side lines, may be up to 2cm higher than the centre but each end should be at the same height.

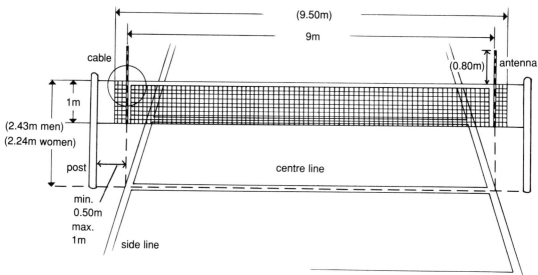

The **posts** which support the net should be rounded and smooth, and they must not present any danger to the players. They need to be adjustable in height and fixed to the floor (without using wires or weights) at a distance of between 50cm and 1m away from the side of the court.

● **THE BALL**

The **ball** itself is made of flexible leather and should be uniform and light in colour; its circumference is between 65 and 67cm and its weight must be in the range 260-280g.

Perhaps the most important measurement, which is always checked just before a game begins, is the pressure – this must be between 0.30 and 0.325kg/cm^2.

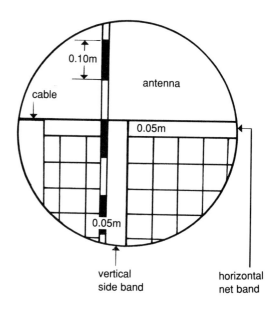

The net and post assembly showing the side bands and antennae. The net is hung directly over the axis of the centre line and the vertical side band is directly over the side line.

● PLAYERS' EQUIPMENT

A player's **equipment** consists of a shirt, shorts and shoes. Shirts and shorts must be uniform and clean – the whole team should wear identical kit in competitive play. Sports shoes must be light and pliable, normally have rubber or synthetic soles and no heels. Players' shirts should be numbered in the centre of the front and back; numbers between 1 and 18 are allowed. The **team captain** should be identified by means of a strip of material underlining the number on the front of the shirt.

The referee can, if asked, permit a player to play barefoot. If the temperature is cold, the teams may be allowed to wear training suits – although the extra clothing must be uniform for the whole team and must also be numbered if the original shirt numbers are covered up. A player is never allowed to wear any object which could cause injury or give an artificial advantage – wristwatches, bracelets, large rings or earrings and heavy decorative chains or necklaces, for example, must all be removed before playing. Any thin, light jewellery, such as small sleeper earrings or gold chains which can be tucked into a shirt or taped up, may be worn if no danger is presented to other players. In such borderline cases a player should be advised that participation is at his or her own risk.

Spectacles can be worn, at a player's own risk; in this case it is advisable to use plastic lenses and to tape the glasses securely around the head, if possible. Contact lenses are allowed but the referee is not permitted to delay a game in order to search for a lost lens! Finally, under no circumstances can a player take part in a game wearing a plaster cast. Protective material is allowed – kneepads, ankle or elbow supports, soft tape around the fingers and so on, but there must be no 'solid' material (metal brace, hard plastic support, etc.) involved.

PARTICIPANTS

● THE TEAMS

A **team** consists of a maximum of 12 players. Since there must at all times be six players on court, this means that there can be up to six **substitute** players available during the game. In addition, there can be three non-playing team members: a **coach**, an **assistant coach** and a **trainer**. Both the captains and coaches of each team must sign the scoresheet before the match; this is done in order to verify the team lists as accurate. Once the scoresheet is signed, the recorded players cannot be changed; only players listed on the scoresheet can take part in the game. (It is common practice for the scorer to rule out any unused boxes in the team sheet, to indicate that players' names cannot be added at a later time.)

The player who signs the scoresheet as captain, and who represents the team when the toss is taken , is called the **team captain**. At all times, a team must have a captain on court; this person is called the **game captain** and is the only player who is permitted to speak to the match officials during the game. Other than the coach, only the game captain can make requests for time-out or substitution; this captain can also ask for equipment to be checked or for the team's positions to be verified.

The team captain functions as the game captain when on court; only if the team captain is substituted off court must another player take over as game captain.

Explanation time: first referee Dudley Williams explains a decision to Malory's Jefferson Williams in a Cup Final. Only the game captain is permitted to speak to the match officials, and then only to obtain a clarification – no argument or prolonged discussion is allowed.

● BEHAVIOUR

Players should know the basic rules of volleyball; they are expected to accept referees' decisions without dispute and must behave respectfully and courteously, not only towards the officials but also towards opponents, team-mates and spectators. Players are not allowed to delay the game unnecessarily, and they may not try to influence the referees' decisions or to intimidate opponents.

If something happens during play which is unclear, the game captain may ask the referee for an explanation but may not argue; if a major disagreement arises then the game captain can ask for this to be recorded as a **protest** on the scoresheet at the end of the game, but the referee's decision stands and

Coaching from the bench. A coach (or any other team member) may give instructions during the match to players on court, but only whilst sitting on the team bench. Here, Great Britain coach Ralph Hippolyte uses this rule to good effect.

the game continues. At the end of the match, each team captain must sign the scoresheet to confirm any protest and to ratify the match result.

The team's captain and coach are jointly responsible for the conduct and discipline of the team members, although during play any team member, whether on court or sitting on the team bench, can give instruction or encouragement to other team members. Bench personnel must, however, remain seated – a coach who stands up to communicate with the players on court should be warned. Equally, instructions cannot be shouted to the opponents, or to the officials!

Other non-playing team personnel – the assistant coach and the trainer, if present – may sit on the team bench but cannot intervene officially during the game. Only if the coach is forced to leave the team may the assistant coach take over the official duties and responsibilities.

All non-playing team members – the coaching staff and the substitutes – normally sit on the team bench, which is located next to the scorer's table, outside the free zone. (In a gymnasium or hall where the team benches are less than 3m away from the side of the court, the free zone is effectively shortened. Although technically illegal, this is a common occurrence in many sports halls.)

When getting ready to go on court a substitute player may warm up in an area in the corner of the sports hall, but a ball may not be used for this purpose except between sets. For important events a special **warm-up area**, measuring approximately 3m × 3m, is marked out on each bench-side corner, outside the free zone.

SCORING SYSTEM

Volleyball is normally played to the best of five sets, i.e. the first team to gain three sets will win the match, although local variations and age or time considerations may affect the rules for specific events. In the first four sets, only the serving team can score a point; in the final set a point is won every time a rally is played, no matter which team served: this is called **rally point**.

A team wins a set when it reaches 15 points, providing it has a two-point lead; without this lead the set continues. Examples of winning set scores would be 15–13, 16–14 or 17–15. (Sets cannot be won with scores of 15–14 or 16–15.) But in the first four sets there is a **point limit** reached at 17 points; if the score reaches 16–16, then the next point will win the set, i.e. at 17–16.

Again, however, the fifth set is different: it has no point limit at seventeen points. To win the fifth set (and hence the match), a team must have a clear two-point lead. Theoretically, therefore, the fifth set could go on to 18–16, 19–17, 20–18 and so on.

PREPARATION FOR PLAY

● THE TOSS

Before the official warm-up, the first referee carries out a **toss** in the presence of the two team captains. The winner of the toss can choose whether to serve or receive service, or can choose on which side of the court the team wishes to play. Whichever captain loses the toss chooses the remaining alternative. If the set score reaches 2–2, another toss is taken before the fifth set.

● THE WARM-UP

In practice, players will be warming up for some time before the match begins. However, the final part of the warm-up, just before the match starts, has a special significance and is called the **warm-up session**, or official warm-up. Each team gets five minutes in which to play over the actual net, although in practice the two teams usually agree to have 10 minutes warm-up at the net together, rather than five minutes each. Exactly how the players use this time is not specified in the rules; this is a matter for mutual agreement between the teams. Only if the teams cannot agree would the referee dictate exactly how the warm-up is conducted. In most domestic competitions, however, the players usually spend most of this time hitting from different positions across the net, with the final couple of minutes used for serving practice.

If either team wishes to have a separate warm-up, then they take it in turns to use the net for five minutes each. During this time the other team must leave the playing court completely. The team that is to serve first in the match must warm up first.

● TEAM STARTING LINE-UP

Before the start of each set, the coach of each team must give to the scorer a **rotation slip** on which the **starting line-up** of the team is listed, in service order. Once this order is recorded on the scoresheet, it cannot be changed until the next set. Just before the set begins, the referees must check to make sure that the correct players are on court; if the players on court do not match exactly the line-up as recorded on the scoresheet then this must be corrected by insisting that the players on court are changed into the correct starting line-up. The only way a coach can change this playing order is by making a legal substitution.

A team that refuses to play, or that is not ready to play by the agreed time, is declared in **default** and will lose the match with a score of 15–0, 15–0, 15–0.

● COURT POSITIONS

At the moment the ball is hit by the server, and only at this moment, all the other players must be standing on the court and in their correct positions; if this is not the case then a fault is committed and the opposing team will win the rally.

The three players who can play at the net are called **front-court** players, and they occupy court positions 4 (on the left), 3 (in the centre) and 2 (on the right). The other three players are **back-court players** and occupy positions 5 (left), 6 (centre) and 1 (right). (The numbering for these positions is the order in which the players of the team will take turns at service.)

At the moment the ball is served, each front-row player must be nearer to the centre line than the corresponding back-row player; thus the player in position 4 must be in front of player 5, player 3 must be in front of player 6 and player 2 must be in front of player 1. These are the possible front/back faults.

Also, at the instant the ball is hit on service, each right (or left) player must be nearer the corresponding side line than the central players. Thus 2 must be to the right of 3 and 4 must be to the left of 3; also 1 must be to the right of 6 and 5 must be to the left of 6. These are the possible sideways faults.

The only exception to this rule is the server (in position 1) , who must be off court and can stand anywhere behind the entire end line, in the service zone. Note that, for the purposes of this rule, the position of a player is determined by the position of feet in contact with the ground.

Once the ball has been served, the

players may move anywhere and take up any position on court or in the free zone.

● ROTATION

When the serving team wins a rally, it scores a point and continues to serve. When the receiving team wins a rally it gains the right to serve next and its players must **rotate**, one position clockwise around the court. In this way the players take it in turns to serve and also to play in front or back court.

● FAULTS

When the wrong player serves (a **rotational fault**), or when two or more players are standing in the wrong positions at the moment of service (a **positional fault**), the team at fault will lose the rally and the fault must be corrected. Also, if the team at fault has scored any points whilst in the wrong rotation, all such points should be cancelled.

Court positions of the front-court and back-court players.

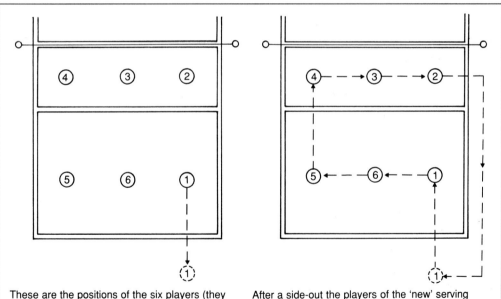

These are the positions of the six players (they are not the players' numbers as they appear on their shirts). Numbers 2, 3 and 4 are front-court players; numbers 5, 6 and 1 are back-court players. If the team is serving then the player at position 1 becomes the server.

After a side-out the players of the 'new' serving team rotate one place in a clockwise direction. The player from position 2 becomes the server and takes up position 1 on the court.

A Examples to illustrate the position between front- and back-line pairs

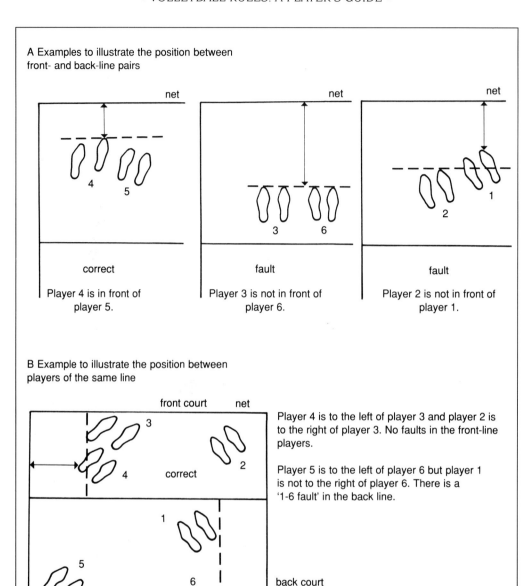

correct

Player 4 is in front of player 5.

fault

Player 3 is not in front of player 6.

fault

Player 2 is not in front of player 1.

B Example to illustrate the position between players of the same line

correct

Player 4 is to the left of player 3 and player 2 is to the right of player 3. No faults in the front-line players.

Player 5 is to the left of player 6 but player 1 is not to the right of player 6. There is a '1-6 fault' in the back line.

fault

back court

Position of players at the moment of service.
A: possible front/back faults;
B: possible sideways faults.

SERVICE

Service is the act of putting the ball into play by the right back-row player (the player in position 1), who hits the ball with one hand or an arm. The ball must be thrown in the air (or released) before being hit; it cannot be served whilst resting on the other hand. At the moment the ball is hit the server must either be standing in, or have just jumped from, the service zone. After hitting the ball the server may step onto the court.

The teams take it in turns to have first service in each set; whichever team starts the first set, the other team will serve first in the second set, and so on. If the match reaches a fifth set then another toss is taken to determine which team will serve first.

The referee should whistle and signal for service as soon as the player is ready, with the ball, and both teams are ready to play. The server then has five seconds in which to serve; failure to do so is a fault and the team will lose service. A service made before the

This is a foot fault on service. At the moment of the service hit, or the take-off for a jump serve, the server must not touch the court (including the end line) or the ground outside the service zone. After the service hit the player may land anywhere.

referee's whistle is not a fault; it is cancelled and should be repeated.

If the served ball touches the net, it is a fault and the team will lose service.

● SERVICE ATTEMPT

If the ball, having been released during the serving action, is allowed to land without touching the server, then this is considered to be a **service attempt.** In this case, the referee must again whistle for service and a second, and final, service action can be made, for which the server is given an additional three seconds only. (This should not be confused with the situation in tennis, where a server is allowed two attempts, even if the first one is struck and goes out or hits the net.)

● SCREENING

A player in the serving team may not deliberately try to prevent the receiving team players from seeing the served ball. A player who waves his/her arms, jumps or moves around in such a way that the opponents are distracted is guilty of the offence of **screening**. When the ball is served over such a player the team will lose service.

A team makes a **collective screen** when the server is hidden behind a group of two or more team-mates and the ball is served over them. This fault is normally called only when the ball is served low over the net, since a ball served high into the air can easily be seen by the receiving players.

Collective screen. Groups of two or more players form a collective screen if they stand in such a way as to prevent players in the receiving team from seeing the service.

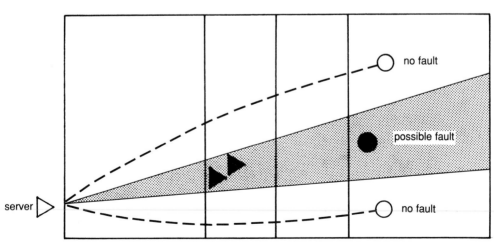

PLAYING THE BALL

● STATES OF PLAY

A rally begins and ends with the referee's whistle. The ball is **in play** from the instant the ball is hit on service and is **out of play** as soon as the ball lands or a fault is committed.

The ball is **in** when it lands on the floor of the playing court, including the boundary lines. If any part of the ball touches any part of a line, it is considered to be 'in'.

The ball is **out** when it lands without touching the court or lines, or if it touches the ceiling or an object outside the court, or if it touches any part of the net outside the vertical side markers.

A ball which touches an antenna – or which would have touched an antenna had it extended to the ceiling – is also considered to be 'out', as is a ball which crosses completely underneath the net.

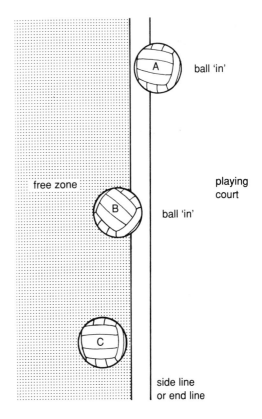

Ball 'in' or 'out'. The ball lands 'in' when any part of it touches the floor of the playing court, including the boundary lines.

● PLAYING FAULTS

Any action contrary to the rules is a **playing fault**; the consequence of a fault is the loss of the rally. If two or more faults are committed successively, only the first one is counted. If two faults are committed by opponents at exactly the same time, a **double fault** is called and the rally must be replayed.

● TEAM HITS

A team is allowed a maximum of three hits, in order to return the ball over the net. For the purposes of this rule, any contact with the **block** (see page 36) does not count as one of the team's three touches. A player cannot touch the ball twice consecutively, i.e. the same player cannot make the first and second (or second and third) of the team's three touches. (There are two exceptions to this, i.e. blocking and **first team contact** – see Ball Contact on page 28.) The same player can, however, make the first and third of the team's three hits.

Held ball. When opposing players make a simultaneous contact over the net and the ball is held between them, this is a double fault and the rally must be replayed.

● SIMULTANEOUS CONTACT

When two opponents touch the ball over the net at exactly the same time, this is called a **simultaneous contact.** If the ball stays in play, the team receiving the ball after such a contact is entitled to three more touches. If such a ball goes 'out', it is a fault against the team on the opposite side.

When two opponents touch the ball at the same time over the net, the ball will often rest in the hands of both players and sometimes a 'pushing contest' begins. This then constitutes a **held ball** (see Ball Contact on page 28) and a double fault should be called. In this case, the rally is replayed.

● ASSISTED HIT

A player cannot take support from any object or person, including a team-mate, in order to reach the ball. Thus it is illegal, for example, to climb on the post or to lift a team-mate when playing the ball; this would constitute the fault of **assisted hit**. This rule applies only to the playing area; anything outside the free zone (for example, the team bench) is excluded from the rule and so could be used to assist the player.

● BALL CONTACT

The ball may be touched by *any* part of the body. Recent rule changes now allow contact with the feet and, although the intention behind the change was to allow more freedom in defensive plays, there is no fault committed if a player kicks the ball deliberately in an attempt to play the ball.

Double contact (or double touch). A double contact is not penalized any time the player is making the first of the team's permitted contacts, providing the player makes only a single action at playing the ball.

The ball must not be caught or thrown; if it is, the fault of **held ball** is committed. This happens when the ball rests momentarily in the hands or on the arms, or is pushed or lifted. This fault is sometimes called a carried ball.

The ball may contact more than one part of the body, provided that these contacts happen at the same time. If they are not simultaneous, the fault of **double contact** (sometimes called double touch) is committed. This is the second type of handling fault, but there are two occasions when this fault is not called. First, whenever a player is making the first of the team's three hits, a double contact is allowed – providing the player makes only a single action at playing the ball. Second, any players taking part in a block are allowed to make more than one contact with the ball, again providing that these touches occur during a single blocking action. (In fact, a player who touches the ball during a block can legally make the next contact as well, since the block itself does not count as one of the three permitted team contacts.)

Playing the ball. When a player is not in a good position to play the ball, there is additional leniency given on ball handling. Here, the player has been forced to move quickly in order to retrieve the ball. First referee Dan Dingle must be slightly less strict in his judgment before calling a handling fault in such circumstances.

When judging handling faults, the referee takes into consideration only the contact between the player and the ball; it should not matter what sound the contact makes, whether the ball spins or whether it travels in the intended direction.

In accordance with recent refereeing instructions from the FIVB, designed to encourage longer rallies and spectacular actions, referees now have a degree of flexibility in calling handling faults. In particular, international referees are instructed to be less severe on the judgment of handling when the player is not in a good position to play the ball. For example, when a player has to move some distance in order to play the ball, or when there is a quick rebound action, the referee will allow more leniency before penalizing handling faults. Even more significantly, the **first team contact** (i.e. whenever a player is making the first of the team's three permitted contacts) may now be made using any technique, unless the ball is actually caught or thrown.

PLAY AT THE NET

● BALL CROSSING THE NET

The ball must pass over the net within the **crossing space**. This is the area above the top of the net and between (but not including) the antennae. The ball is permitted to touch the net whilst crossing it, except on service. The ball is also allowed to rebound from the net, in between the vertical side markers, and be played again, providing the team has not already used its three permitted hits. A ball which has partially crossed the plane of the net, either underneath or outside the crossing space, can be played back into court. Even if the ball has completely crossed the plane of the net, outside the crossing space, it can still be played back, within the team's three hits, providing that the player does not touch the opponents' court.

● PLAYER TOUCHING THE NET

Players are not normally allowed to touch the net during play; an exception to this is when a player who is not involved in trying to play the ball makes a slight contact with the net accidentally; in such cases, no fault is committed. It should be stressed that any kind of action at the net – jumping, landing, attempting to play the ball (even if no contact is made) or even pretending to play the ball – will all be considered as playing actions here, and hence a player who touches the net during any of these actions will still be penalized for making contact with the net. Only those slight contacts where a player is not involved *in any way* with playing the ball may be considered exempt from this rule; in

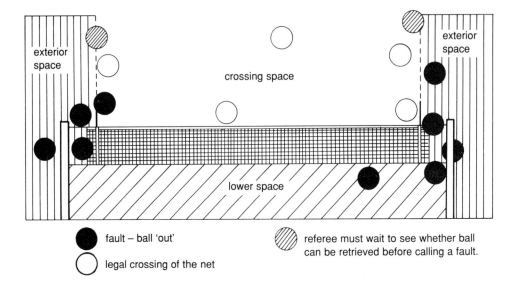

● fault – ball 'out'

◯ legal crossing of the net

▨ referee must wait to see whether ball can be retrieved before calling a fault.

practice, most contacts with the net will continue to be called as faults.

It is never a fault if a player touches the posts, ropes, cables or any other object outside the 9.50m length of the net. Also, it is not a fault if the net moves and touches a player, for example, if the ball is driven into the net and this causes the net to touch a player standing close to it.

Crossing space. During play (except on service), the ball may touch the net inside the antennae (including the vertical side bands), but not the antenna itself or the net outside it.

● BLOCKER REACHING OVER THE NET

In blocking, a player is allowed to reach completely over the net and make contact with the ball, but only if this does not interfere with the opponents' attack. One example of this

Reaching beyond the net is permitted only if there is no interference with the opponent's attempts to play the ball.

Putting a foot on (or over) the centre line is not a fault, providing some part of the foot remains in contact with the line or directly above it. It is only a fault if the entire foot crosses completely over the line.

would be where the opposing team has already made three contacts; in this case, no further contact is possible and so a blocker would be allowed to reach completely over the net and play the ball. Even after the first or second hit, however, it might be possible to block over the net – but only if, in the opinion of the referee, no player from the attacking team could possibly have reached the ball before it would have crossed the net.

● PLAYERS UNDER THE NET

A player can put feet and hands on and over the centre line, providing that some part of the foot or hand remains in contact with the line or directly above it. It is only a fault if the entire foot or hand crosses completely over this line. Note, however, that this does not apply to any other part of the body; for example, it is a fault if the knee touches the opponents' court even slightly over the centre line.

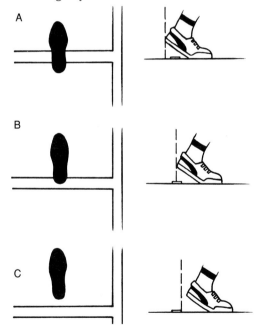

A, B Legal (even if the foot is partly off the ground)
C Fault

Foot over centre line. Some part of the foot must stay in contact with the line or be directly above it.

33

● THE ATTACK-HIT

Any action which directs the ball towards the opponents' court, however this is made, is considered to be an **attack-hit.** (Special rules govern the service and the block, so these actions are usually considered separately.)

A front-row player can carry out an attack-hit from any part of the court and with the ball at any height, providing of course that the ball is still on the player's own side of the net. Thus there are no restrictions on the type of hit which can be made by a front-court player.

A back-court player can only attack the ball under certain circumstances; first, if the player is standing in the back court (i.e. behind the attack-line) then an attack-hit is always permitted. This applies even if the player jumps from behind the attack-line, hits the ball and lands in the front zone: such a play is perfectly legal. Second, even if the back-court player is clearly standing in the front zone, an attack-hit can still be made if the ball is not completely above the level of the top of the net.

A third consideration for the referee concerns whether the ball travels

Richard Dobell (2) sets overhead for Great Britain against Poland, as Marcus Russell (6) makes a 'feint' attack. Both players are considered part of the action of attempting to play the ball, and so neither is allowed to make any contact with the net.

directly towards the net after such a back-court hit; the back-court hit is a fault only if the attack is **completed**, i.e. the ball crosses over the net or goes into a block. (The referee can therefore penalize this fault only once the direction of the ball is known and not at the moment the ball is contacted.)

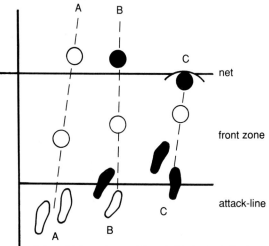

A Legal (player jumped from behind attack-line)
B Fault (player's foot on or over attack-line)
C Fault (even though ball was blocked before it crossed the net)

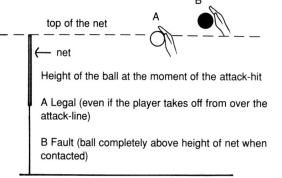

Height of the ball at the moment of the attack-hit

A Legal (even if the player takes off from over the attack-line)

B Fault (ball completely above height of net when contacted)

Attack-hit by back-line player from the front zone.

Back-row player's attack-hit. Matthew Jones attacks from the back court for Great Britain. The player must take off from behind the attack line, but can land anywhere on court afterwards.

If a back-court player directs the ball towards the opponents, whilst in the front zone and making contact with the ball when it is completely above the height of the top of the net, the fault of **illegal back-court attack-hit** is committed and this is penalized as soon as the ball crosses over the net or is touched by an opponents' block.

● THE BLOCK

Blocking is the action made by players standing close to the net who try to intercept the ball coming from the opponents' side by placing their hands or arms over the top of the net. The blocking action is often made without actually touching the ball; this is called a **block attempt**. If a blocker actually touches the ball during the blocking action, this is called a **completed block**.

Sometimes, two (or even three) players will jump together and make a blocking action; this is permitted but will be considered as a **collective block** only if the players are close to each other.

If this is the case, the rule which allows blockers to make more than one

Players 1 and 2 are not close to each other. If the ball is touched by player 1 and then by player 2, only the first touch is counted as a block – player 2 will be making the first of the team's three allowed hits.

Players 3 and 4 form a collective block. If they both touch the ball, the team will still have three more hits.

touch of the ball will apply to all players in the block; hence the ball may contact players in the block several times in quick succession; the team will still be entitled to three more hits after such a play, since the block does not count as one of the team's three permitted contacts.

The first touch after a block (i.e. the first of the team's three hits) can be made by any player, including the one who may have just touched the ball in the block.

Collective block. Two or three front-court players can make a collective block, if they jump close together. The ball can make multiple contacts on the block, providing there is only a single action made by the players. After the block contact(s), the team is still entitled to three more hits to return the ball.

Collective block. To be considered as a collective block, the players must be close to the net and close to each other.

A back-court player is not permitted to take part in a block; if this happens and any contact with the ball is made, then the fault of **illegal block** is committed, even if the back-court player was not the one who touched the ball. In effect, a back-court player jumping at the net makes the whole block illegal, if there is any contact with the ball.

It is not permitted for a player to block the service. In fact, it is not allowed to return the service directly to the opponents at all if contact is made in the front zone and from above the height of the net.

STOPPAGES

● **SUBSTITUTION**

Substitution is the act of exchanging two players; one player comes off court and is replaced by someone from the team bench. A team is allowed to have up to six substitutions per set, and it is possible to replace more than one player at the same time. For example, a coach may ask for a double substitution, taking two players off and putting two players on, but this will count as two of the six permitted substitutions. (All six players could be changed at one request; unusual but possible.)

A player who starts a set may be substituted off court and later may return, but this can happen only once during the same set, i.e. the player can go off and come back, and that's it for the set. Note also that the player must replace the one who originally substituted; for example, if player number 5 is taken off and replaced by player number 4, then it must be player number 4 who gets taken off when player 5 returns.

Likewise, a player who starts the set sitting on the team bench may go on during the set and can then be taken off again, but only once during the same set. In this way, a substitute and the original player are paired for the duration of a set.

When the request for a substitution is made, the player(s) concerned must be ready to enter the court, standing in the substitution zone; if this is not the case a team may be penalized for delaying the game.

Substitution of players. A team can change more than one player at a time, providing the coach makes this clear at the time of the request. Here, second referee Denis Le Breuilly controls a double exchange of players, one after the other, ensuring that the scorer is able to record both substitutions correctly.

● EXCEPTIONAL SUBSTITUTION

A player who is injured and cannot continue should be legally substituted. If this is not possible, the team is allowed to make an 'illegal' substitution – in this case, called an **exceptional substitution**.

A player who is sent off – either expelled for the set or disqualified for the whole match – must also be legally substituted; a team cannot continue playing with fewer than six players. If, however, no legal substitute is available then the team is not allowed to make an exceptional substitution and it becomes **incomplete**, either for the set or for the match. In these circumstances, the opponents will be awarded the points, or the points and sets, needed to win the set or the match.

● ILLEGAL SUBSTITUTION

If a team is found to have made an illegal substitution, the fault is penalized with the loss of the rally. The illegal substitution must be corrected and the team at fault will lose any points it has scored whilst the illegal player was on court.

● REQUESTS FOR STOPPAGES

Requests for substitution or time-out may be made only by the coach or the game captain and only when the ball is out of play and before the whistle for service. The request can be made to either the first referee or the second referee (see page 47), and at the time of the request the correct signal must be given by the coach or captain concerned.

● TIME-OUT

A team is entitled to request up to two time-outs per set. Each time-out lasts for 30 seconds and a team may, if it wishes, take the second time-out immediately after the first. During a time-out the players should leave the court and go to the team bench.

● IMPROPER REQUESTS

An **improper** request for stoppage is one which is made by the wrong person, or at the wrong time, or if the team has already had its permitted number. In such cases there is no penalty and the request is simply refused, providing the game is not delayed. If the game is delayed unnecessarily when an improper request is made, then the team will be sanctioned by the award of a **delay warning**.

If a team repeats an improper request during the same set, it will automatically be deemed guilty of delaying the game, irrespective of whether there is any actual delay or not. The team is sanctioned, in the first instance by the award of a **delay warning** (yellow card). Any further improper requests during the same set will result in the team being sanctioned with the award of a **delay penalty** (red card).

● INJURY

If a serious accident occurs then the referee should stop play so that the injury can be assessed; this rally is then replayed. If an injured player cannot be substituted, either legally or exceptionally, then a three-minute recovery period is allowed. (This will be the case only if the team has just six players and no substitutes at all.) This recovery period is permitted only once per player; if the player does not recover within three minutes, the team will be declared incomplete and will lose the set (and match, if the player is still unable to start the following set).

● INTERVALS BETWEEN SETS

All intervals between sets last three minutes. After each set the teams change ends, except in the deciding (fifth) set, when a new toss is taken to determine who serves and at which ends the teams play. In the deciding set, the teams also change ends when one of them reaches eight points. If this change is not made at the proper time, it will take place as soon as the error is noticed.

DELAYS AND MISCONDUCT

● DELAYS TO THE GAME

Actions of players that delay the game are sanctioned with delay warnings and delay penalties. Examples include taking too long to make a substitution, not coming back on court immediately after the end of a time-out, not rolling the ball back at the end of a rally and so on. On the first occasion this happens in a set, the referee gives a **delay warning** against the team. This is not a sanction on an individual player: it is given against the whole team and warns all players against a repetition. The sanction is indicated when the referee hold a **yellow card** up to the wrist (presumably indicating an imaginary wristwatch!), and this sanction is not to be confused with the award of a yellow card as a personal misconduct warning – see next section. If any player in the same team delays play for a second time in the same set, a **delay penalty** is given against the team; this has the effect of losing a rally. This is shown by pointing the **red card** at the wrist. If the team was serving, it will lose service; if it was receiving service at the time of the offence, the opponents will score a point. For every additional time a player of the same team delays the game in the same set, another delay penalty is given, with the same effect. Players cannot be sent off for delaying the game.

● MISCONDUCT

Misconduct is defined as any kind of personal incorrect behaviour towards the officials, opponents, spectators or, in some cases, even team-mates. As with delaying the game, misconduct is sanctioned by using the red and yellow

Misconduct Sanction Scale

Categories	Times	Sanction	Cards to show	Consequence
1 Unsportsmanlike conduct	First	Warning	Yellow	Prevention: no penalty
	Second	Penalty	Red	Loss of a rally
	Third	Expulsion	Both jointly	Expulsion from the playing court for the set
2 Rude conduct	First	Penalty	Red	Loss of a rally
	Second	Expulsion	Both jointly	Expulsion from the playing court for the set
3 Offensive conduct	First	Disqualification	Both separately	Expulsion from the playing area and the team bench for the match
4 Aggression				

cards, but the similarity ends there. Whereas delaying play is a **team** offence, misconduct is dealt with on a **personal** basis, i.e. it is the individual team member who is punished, rather than the whole team. All members of the team – including the coach and other non-playing personnel – are governed by the same disciplinary system.

There are three basic categories of misconduct:

Unsportsmanlike conduct This is the least serious offence, for minor acts of misbehaviour such as arguing with officials, trying to intimidate opponents and so on. On the first occasion this happens, the referee will show the yellow card and this is called a **misconduct warning** against the player. The effect of this card is to warn the player concerned not to repeat any misbehaviour during the same match. Apart from this, the warning has no effect on the game.

Rude conduct This is a more serious offence and results in the award of a

misconduct penalty against the team member, shown by the referee as a red card. When this happens, the player's team effectively loses a rally as a result. If they were serving, service is lost; if they were receiving service, the opponents will score a point as a result of the red card being shown. There are two ways to get a red card. One is for a major offence which shows contempt or a total lack of respect for the way the game should be played – for example, kicking the ball angrily into the crowd after losing a point: the referee should award a misconduct penalty straightaway, without any need for a previous warning. A red card can also be shown, however, if a player commits a minor offence after having already had a warning. It is not possible to give the same player two yellow cards in the same match; for the second minor offence the referee must show the red card.

Offensive or **aggressive conduct** If a player makes a physical attack on another participant, or even an intended aggressive act, the sanction is immediate **disqualification.** No previous warning is required and the player concerned must leave the court and the playing area for the rest of the match. A disqualified player cannot stay in the warm-up area or sit on the team bench; effectively, the player must leave the sports hall and takes no further part in the match. The referee indicates a disqualification by holding up red and yellow cards, in separate hands. When this happens, the team itself is not penalized, i.e. the service is not lost and no point is awarded to the opponents.

There is a fourth sanction available to the referee, for when a player is guilty of further misconduct in a set, after having already been shown the red card. This is an **expulsion**, and the player is sent off for the remainder of the set in progress. Again this involves leaving the playing area altogether but, unlike a total disqualification, the player is allowed to return to the game for the following set(s).

As a general rule, players start each new match with a clean sheet, but during any particular match the sanctions build up progressively if misconduct is repeated. A player cannot be shown two yellow cards in the same match; a repetition of unsportsmanlike conduct gets a red card. Similarly, a player cannot get two red cards in the same set; repetition of rude conduct causes the player to be expelled for the set – the referee indicates this by showing the red and yellow cards in the same hand.

If a team member is guilty of misconduct in between sets, i.e. during the set interval, then any punishment applies for the following set.

THE OFFICIALS

The team of officials for a volleyball match consists of:

- the **first referee**
- the **second referee**
- the **scorer**
- the **line judges**

For high-profile matches such as Internationals, Cup Finals and some top-division games, there may also be a team of (usually six) **ball-retrievers** whose job it is to avoid delays by ensuring there is always a ball ready for the server at each end. This requires more than one match ball and, for obvious reasons, is called the three-ball system. In really big games there may also be a team of two or three floor moppers, whose job it is to wipe damp, sweaty patches from the floor, to reduce the danger of injury to the players.

The 'team' of officials can therefore range from just a single person (who referees, scores and line judges) to a squad of over 15 people!

● THE FIRST REFEREE

The first referee directs the match from start to finish and is in overall control of the game, having authority over all of the other match officials and the ability to overrule decisions made by any other official if these are thought to be incorrect. As is usual in many sports, the referee has the power to decide upon all matters which may arise, including those not specifically covered in the rules. In extreme circumstances, for example, the first referee can replace any other officials who do not perform their duties properly.

Before the game begins the first referee inspects the playing area and equipment, takes the toss with the two team captains, briefs the other officials on their duties and controls the teams' official warm-up period at the net.

Location of match officials.

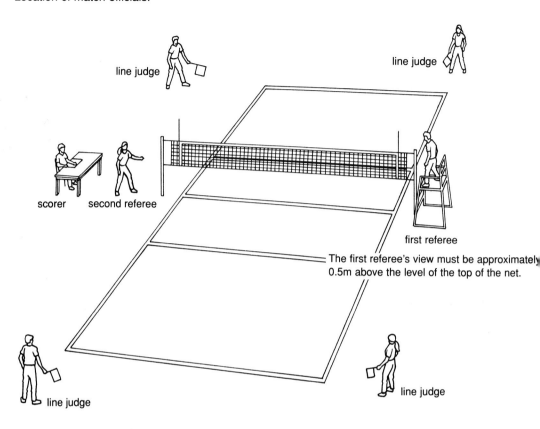

The first referee's view must be approximately 0.5m above the level of the top of the net.

During the game the first referee is situated on a stand or raised platform at one end of the net; the first referee's view must be approximately 50cm above the level of the top of the net. Decisions are communicated by means of the whistle and hand signals; it is not usually necessary for the referee to communicate verbally.

The first referee gives the signal which authorizes the service and begins each rally; during the match only the first referee can sanction misconduct or delay (i.e. award red and yellow cards), and only the first referee is authorized to decide upon:

• faults of the server or the serving team
• faults in playing the ball (handling errors)
• faults above the net.

If any clarification is required during the game, this should be done only by the game captain speaking to the first referee, who should give a brief explanation or interpretation of the rules when asked. However, no argument or prolonged discussion should be permitted; if the captain is not satisfied with the explanation given, a **protest** can be lodged at the end of the game but play continues and the immediate decision of the first referee is final. If the captain still wishes to record the protest at the end of the match, a brief description of the facts can be written on the scoresheet and the incident will be referred to the league or event organizers for adjudication.

● THE SECOND REFEREE

The second referee is an assistant to the first referee but also has a range of specific responsibilities. These duties are carried out standing at the post on the opposite side of the net to, and facing, the first referee.

Before the start of each set (and whenever necessary at other times) the second referee is responsible for checking that the positions of the players on court correspond to the official line-up sheet.

During the match, the second referee is empowered to whistle and signal faults involving:-

- positional faults of the team receiving service
- players touching the net
- players crossing over the centre line

- back-court players (making attack-hits or blocking)
- a ball touching an antenna or going over the net outside the legal crossing space.

In addition, the second referee may signal (without whistling) any faults which are technically the responsibility of the first referee. This is usually done only if there is reason to believe that the first referee has not seen the fault, and even then the second referee may not insist – the first referee cannot be overruled! The signals most commonly used by the first and second referees are illustrated.

There are specific technical duties carried out by the second referee, including:

- controlling the work of the scorer
- supervising the behaviour of the team members on the benches
- controlling substitute players in the warm-up areas
- checking the floor condition during play and supervising floor-wiping
- ensuring that the match balls stay within specifications.

Either of the two referees can authorize time-outs, although in practice it is the second referee who times their duration and controls behaviour during the stoppage. Similarly, either referee can authorize a substitution, but it is the second referee who supervises the exchange of players. The second referee is responsible for reminding each coach

Referee's signals

team to serve next

positional fault

change court

time-out

ball 'in'

ball 'out'

misconduct

ball held

end of set

double contact

delay in service

four contacts

net touched
by a player

double fault

reaching beyond
the net

blocking fault
or screening

ball touched

substitution

team delay

back-court attack-hit

service authorization

crossing the centre line
(or ball underneath net)

(and the first referee) when the teams have had their second time-out in a set, and also when they have had either five or six substitutions; this, and the need to check on players' positions, involves close liaison with the scorer at all times.

If the first referee should become ill or indisposed, the second referee must accept overall control for the match.

opposite side of the court to, and facing, the first referee. This position directly behind the second referee makes it easier for these two officials to cooperate.

Before the game begins the scorer registers all the match details – date, venue, teams etc. – on the scoresheet and obtains the signatures of the captains and coaches. Signing not only confirms the identities of team captains and coaches, it is also taken as verification of the correct identity,

● THE SCORER

The scorer is responsible for filling in the match scoresheet as the game progresses. To do this, the scorer sits at the scorer's table located on the

The start of the rally. The first referee authorizes the service and watches the serving team for service errors, positional faults and possible screening. The second referee watches the positions of the receiving players.

shirt number and eligibility of each player in the team. Before each set the scorer must get the team line-up from each coach.

During the match the scorer must record on the scoresheet the points scored, the time-outs and substitutions, and any sanctions which are awarded against the players. In addition, the scorer controls the serving order of each team and tells the referees immediately if the wrong player serves.

The scorer also reminds the second referee of the number of substitutions and time-outs each team has requested, and must inform the referees of any requests by the team captains or coaches which are improper or illegal.

Most important, the scorer must ensure that the visual scoreboard always shows the correct match score. If there should arise any discrepancy between the visual scoreboard and the match scoresheet, it is the scoresheet which is taken as the correct record of the match.

At the end of the match the scorer records the final result, signs the scoresheet and obtains the signatures of both team captains to verify the result and then passes the scoresheet to the referees for checking and final ratification. Each referee signs the scoresheet and nothing further may then be added.

● THE LINE JUDGES

In major competitions, four line judges are compulsory; elsewhere it is acceptable to play with two line judges, although this makes the task more difficult. Some matches take place with no line judges at all – in such cases, the first referee makes all decisions on line calls.

When four line judges are used they stand one in each corner, positioned as if on an imaginary extension of each side line and end line; in this case each line judge is responsible for a single line.

When only two line judges are used, they stand diagonally opposite each other and each watches two lines (the nearest side line and end line).

Line judges should stand about 2m away from each corner of the court; they perform their duties by means of flag signals. Whilst their main duty is to signal whether a ball lands 'in' or 'out' of court, they also signal if they see a ball which has been 'touched' on its way out of court.

Depending upon the experience of the line judges, they can also be asked to signal when the ball crosses the net outside the legal crossing space, or if it touches an antenna, or if there are foot faults on service.

FREQUENTLY ASKED QUESTIONS

When a ball lands 'half in, half out', what happens?
The ball is 'in' when any part of it touches the line.

Is a player allowed to wear tracksuit 'bottoms' on court?
Technically, no. Extra clothing can be worn, when the temperature is low, but the team must still be in uniform (i.e. all players should be the same) and shirt numbers must remain visible.

What happens if a player does not (or cannot) remove a small piece of jewellery?
It can be taped for safety and the player is allowed to play at his/her own risk. If the referee considers the jewellery to be dangerous, the player may be prevented from taking part in the game.

If a team isn't sure who should serve next, what do they do?

The captain can ask for clarification of positions, but the game should not be delayed.

When the team captain goes off court, someone else must take over as game captain; what happens when the team captain comes back?
It will be assumed that the original team captain will resume the captaincy.

Is coaching from the bench allowed?
Yes, providing the coach remains seated.

Can players on the bench shout whether the ball is going to land 'in' or 'out'?
Yes, this counts as coaching and is permitted, provided the players remain on the team bench. But note that they would not be permitted to do this for the opponents!

Can players ask the referee to explain decisions?

Only the captain can speak to the referee, to ask for a clarification.

How is the ten minutes warm-up used?

In whatever way the teams agree. This is not the referee's decision; all the referee does is to time the warm-up and ensure that there is no misconduct or danger to players when both teams warm up at the net together. Usually, teams use the 10 minute period to practise hitting and serving.

Can the coach change a line-up sheet after it has been handed in?

Once the scorer has written a team's starting line-up on the scoresheet, the only way it can be changed is by making a legal substitution.

Can a match continue with five players, if someone is injured?

No, there must be six players at all times. A player who is injured is replaced by a legal substitute; if one is not available, the team can use an 'illegal' player as a substitute. Therefore the only way a team can become incomplete due to injury (and forfeit the match) is if it has only six players to begin with.

Can a match continue with five players, if someone is sent off?

No, there must always be six players on court. A player who is expelled (or disqualified) must be replaced by a legal substitute; if one is not available then the team is incomplete and will lose the set (or match).

Players have to be in certain positions only at the moment of service; does this mean they can move anywhere on court, as soon as the service is made?

Yes, but back-court players are still restricted in terms of how they can play the ball when they are in the front zone.

What happens when the wrong player serves?

Ideally, this fault should be noticed straightaway; as soon as the ball is hit the referee should whistle and award a 'side out' to the opponents. The team should be told which player should have served.

What if the referees don't realize the wrong player has served?

It is really the scorer's job to check rotation, but if this is not done properly the referee must correct the fault as soon as it is spotted. The team at fault will lose any points it has scored whilst the wrong player was serving.

If the scorer notices that the wrong player is about to serve, should the team be told?

No, the scorer permits the fault to be committed and immediately informs the second referee.

Can you have a second attempt at service?

Yes and no. If the first service goes 'out', service is lost and there is no second attempt. But if a player throws the ball up and decides not to hit it, a second and final attempt is allowed, providing the ball was allowed to fall directly to the ground and did not touch the server. (Definitely no second attempt is allowed in beach volleyball.)

From how far off court can a player serve?

As far as the free zone allows, providing the two ends are symmetrical and the floor surface is the same.

Can service be received with a volley?

Yes, there is no reason why not. The normal rules on first team contact apply, i.e. a double touch is allowed (providing only a single action is made by the player) and the ball is not actually caught or thrown.

When is a double contact not penalized?

First, a player who is blocking at the net is allowed to contact the ball more than once. Also, a player who is making the first of the team's three touches may make a double touch, providing that this is done in a single action (i.e. the player does not make a second, different action to play the ball). Finally, it is now the practice for referees to allow a player who is under duress (for example, running to make a difficult defensive play) more leeway and not to call minor handling faults in such circumstances.

Can a player put a foot on the team bench whilst playing the ball?

Yes, since the bench is (by definition) outside the free zone.

Can a player kick the ball deliberately during play?

Yes, technically this is legal, in an attempt to play the ball.

A player jumps to block and lands on an opponent's foot, which is partly across the centre line; is this a fault?

Both players are allowed to place feet on the centre line; only if the referee judges that this action is done deliberately should it be penalized. A player who places a foot completely across the centre line and makes contact with an opponent could be judged to be interfering with play.

A player jumps at the net in an attempt to block but does not touch the ball; on landing, the player makes a slight contact with the net – is this a fault?

Yes. The take-off, block attempt and landing are all considered part of the action of playing the ball.

Two players – one of them a back-court player – jump together at the net in a blocking action. Only the

front-court player touches the ball; is this legal?

No; the back-court player makes the whole block illegal, if either player touches the ball.

A back-court player jumps from behind the attack-line, hits the ball above the net and lands in the front zone; is this legal?

Yes. It is the position of take-off, not landing, which counts.

Can a back-court player ever play the ball back over the net, when standing in the front zone?

Yes, if part of the ball is below the level of the top of the net when the ball is contacted.

When can a player reach over the net?

If there is no contact with the ball and no interference with the opponents' attempts to play the ball. Even if the ball is touched, it may not be a fault; it depends on whether the referee thinks there is any interference to the opponents' attack.

Can a player's feet go over the centre line?

Partly over (either on the ground or in the air) – yes; completely over – no.

Can any ball be blocked?

No, the service cannot be blocked. Also, players in the block cannot reach over the net and interfere with an opponent's attempt to play the ball.

Can players run outside the free zone to play the ball?

Yes, providing the ball has not touched the wall, floor, roof or any other object, a player can move anywhere in an attempt to play the ball.

What happens if the teams do not change ends at eight points in the final set?

Nothing – the teams change ends as soon as the error is noticed and the score stays the same.

Can a coach have a time-out, and then ask for another one straightaway?

Yes, assuming the team still has two time-outs left in the set.

Can a coach make a substitution, and then ask for another one straightaway?

No; play must resume before another request for substitution. If a coach wishes to make two (or more) substitutions, these must be requested at the same time.

If the coach calls for a substitution but the substitute isn't ready, what happens?

The team receives a delay warning, and the substitution is not allowed.

How many substitutions can be made at one time?

Anywhere between one and six, if the team hasn't already had any in the set. But the coach must indicate, at the time of the request, how many players are to be changed – otherwise only one is allowed.

What is a referee's time-out?
Technically, there is no such thing. A three-minute recovery period for injury is allowed, but only for a team with only six players.

Can the coach ask for a time-out just before the service is made?
Not if the referee has already whistled to authorize the service; such a request should be refused, without penalty. However, a coach who deliberately waits until the very last moment before the referee whistles for service, before asking for a time-out or a substitution, could be sanctioned for delaying the game if the request causes any confusion.

Can a team shorten a time-out, if it wishes?
No, a time-out lasts 30 seconds and both teams must stay off court for the whole time.

Just before service a player asks permission to tie a shoelace; what should the referee do?
The game cannot be delayed in this way; technically, the player should receive a delay warning.

A player notices an area of dampness on the court; can the referee be asked for time to mop this up, in case of accident?

Technically, no; a player who waits until just before service to make such a request can be sanctioned for delaying the game. The ideal situation is for the player to dry the area immediately, using a small personal towel (or sometimes the kneepads!). In severe cases, where there is clear danger to players (and especially in the front zone) the referee can allow a small delay to have the court dried properly, using towels from the side of court. But a player should not ask for this; the towel should be fetched immediately at the end of the previous rally and the delay minimized; the second referee should supervise this process and ensure there is no gamesmanship.

What is the punishment for players who shout or act aggressively through the net, in an attempt to intimidate the opponents?
Misconduct warning (yellow card) in the first instance.

Can a player get two yellow cards for misconduct during the same match?
No. The second offence receives a penalty (red card).

Can a player get two red cards for misconduct during the same set?
No. The second offence receives an expulsion for the set.

What is the difference between expulsion and disqualification?

Expulsion is for the remainder of the set; disqualification is for the rest of the match. Also, a player can be expelled only if a penalty (red card) has already been given in the set, whereas a disqualification can be made, without prior sanction, for a serious offence.

Can the referee ask a player if the ball was touched on the way out?

No, it is bad practice for a referee to ask players whether they touched the ball or the net, or if they made any other kind of fault. The referee must make a judgement only on what is actually seen by the match officials; a good referee will always glance towards the second referee and the line judges before making such a decision, to check whether they are signalling any faults.

BEACH VOLLEYBALL

● HISTORY

Beach volleyball developed in the 1920s, on the beaches of Southern California. Originally it was played as the six-a-side indoor game, only outdoors on sand. The game evolved various formats, including four-a-side, until the now familiar two-a-side version became the main competitive event recognized the world over and played on the professional circuits.

As its popularity increased and beach volleyball (sometimes called sand volleyball) spread worldwide, the FIVB promoted the Beach World Series and there is also an established European Grand Prix; even countries without a coastline manage to host major tournaments, and serious players and organizers can import sand in order to train indoors! The recognition of beach volleyball as a sport in its own right was complete in 1996 when it was included for the first time in the Olympic Games.

The rules of beach volleyball have also evolved, as the differing needs of the two-a-side game have dictated changes in order to preserve the game's spectacular, exciting nature.

● RULES OF BEACH VOLLEYBALL

There are many similarities between the rules of beach volleyball and those of the indoor game; the two are, after

Beach volleyball. An alternative game, played two-a-side on sand. Amanda Glover and Audrey Cooper, Great Britain's representatives in the 1996 Olympic Games, in action during the English Beach Grand Prix circuit.

all, both volleyball! The differences which do exist fall into two broad categories – the noticeable distinctions , and the less obvious differences.

Amongst the fundamental differences are the facts that beach volleyball has only two players per team (as opposed to six), the game is played on sand (instead of on wooden or synthetic surfaces), there is no attack-line on court (and hence no need to distinguish between front-court and back-court players) and the players change ends every four or five points (instead of every set).

Less obvious differences include the fact that the players can stand anywhere on court; they are not restricted to certain positions at the moment of service, although the principle of rotation is preserved as the players must take turns to serve.

Players' equipment is less strictly controlled; shirts are optional for men and the players can wear hats and sunglasses if they wish; approved footwear is optional.

Matches can be played over a one-set format (first team to reach 15 points with a two-point lead, point limit at seventeen points) or a two-set format (first to reach 12 points wins the set; if set score reaches one each, a tie-break set is played using rally-point scoring).

There are four time-outs (each 30 seconds) per set, plus every four or five points (when the teams change ends) a further 30 seconds is available.

The way the ball is played in beach volleyball is also slightly different from the indoor game; for a start the ball has a lower internal pressure (0.175–0.225kg/cm^2) which means that it does not travel as fast as in the indoor game, and is more controllable.

Different handling techniques are employed, with a greater flexibility allowed, especially in the reception phase of the game; open hands can be used to receive the ball and the ball may be held slightly without penalty, especially when the player is playing the ball from a difficult position.

Conversely, there are some restrictions which do not apply in the indoor game; for example, the ball cannot be volleyed back over the net unless it is played in a direction at right angles to the shoulders; this prevents feint attacks and means that the ball can be volleyed only straight in front or directly overhead. The hard-hit attack shot is the same in both games, but in beach volleyball the soft-hit 'spike' attack is strictly controlled and is normally made with the heel of the hand, the knuckles or stiff fingers; directing the ball with fingers (the tip, which is allowed in the indoor game) is not permitted. Also, the service may not be received using a volley pass; this is increasingly popular in the indoor game but is penalized on sand.

Other differences in the beach game include the following:

• no coaching is allowed

- the block is counted as one of the team's three hits; only two more hits allowed after a block
- only one attempt at service is allowed; when the ball is thrown up, it must be hit first time
- no centre line is marked and players can go 'under the net', but only providing they do not interfere with the opponents.

In general, the whole game is played on the beach with more flexibility, a more relaxed attitude towards discipline and significantly less formality and protocol than the indoor game. The environment of sun, sea and sand is one of enjoyment and expression, and the popularity of this version of the game continues to increase.

MINI VOLLEYBALL

● HISTORY

Although a simple game in principle, volleyball requires techniques which can be difficult to master, especially for young players using adult equipment on a full-size playing court.

The game of mini volleyball (also called minivolley) was devised specifically for children of around nine to 13 years old, to be introduced into the school curriculum so that the basic skills and techniques of volleyball could be developed in a more appropriate way than with the traditional six-a-side version, for which children in this age group have neither the strength nor the coordination skills required.

With fewer players in a team each player has more ball contact than in the adult game, leading to a greater sense of initial involvement and a faster acquisition of the basic skills.

A smaller court gives success to the team with better ball-control and more agile movement, rather than to those with greater power and strength. Although the point-winning smash can play a part in the later development of play, more often the rallies are long and exciting with the basic skills of movement, service and volley or dig passes being more important.

The first World Minivolley Symposium was held in 1975; since then, many of the world's most successful volleyball nations have implemented a mini volleyball development programme.

● RULES OF MINI VOLLEYBALL

The basic rules and principles of minivolley are the same as for the adult six-a-side game; what differences exist are largely concerned with modifications to the equipment and facilities, where there is more flexibility allowed with respect to the age, strength, height and ability of the players.

Each team has three (sometimes four) players, instead of six. (The game can be introduced in one-a-side or two-a-side format, but competitive play is usually in teams of three.) In addition, up to three additional players are usually allowed in the team, instead of the usual maximum of six substitutes.

The recommended court size is 9m long and 6m wide; this is one-third of the full size and means that minivolley courts can fit sideways across a standard volleyball court. Although this is the ideal size for competition, existing markings can be used to produce courts anywhere between 9m to 12m long and 4.50m to 6m wide. Within reason, minivolley can be played almost anywhere – in the garden, on the beach, in a field or in a school gymnasium or sports hall.

The attack-line dividing front and back zones of court is usually marked at a distance 1.50m or 2m (instead of 3m) from the centre line.

The net is lower for minivolley, according to the height of the players; the ideal height is 2.10m but anywhere between 2m and 2.20m is permitted.

The ball is a critically important factor for young players; using a normal volleyball can sting the wrists and lead to disillusionment. For practice, any suitably light, soft ball is allowed and for introduction to the game a foam ball is ideal. At the stage where competitive matches are being played an approved mini volleyball, made specially for the purpose, is recommended.

The principle of clockwise rotation is preserved in minivolley; the three players are divided into two front-court players (positions 2 and 3) and a back-court player (in position 1). Service is made by the player in position 1, who can serve from anywhere.

After service, the back-court player is forbidden from playing the ball back over the net during a rally whilst standing in the front zone, unless the ball is below the height of the net.

The number of time-outs is the same in minivolley as in the adult game; the maximum number of substitutions, however, is limited to three per team per set (instead of six).

Scoring is the same in mini volleyball, except that matches are usually played to the best of three sets instead of five, i.e. the first team to win two sets wins the match.

Matches are usually controlled by a single referee and a scorer. In minivolley, one of the most important functions of the referee is to ensure that the match is played in a sporting spirit; players are required to demonstrate sportsmanship and cooperation, and should not forget that the opponent is a friend and a playmate.

STANDING AND SITTING VOLLEYBALL

● VOLLEYBALL FOR PEOPLE WITH DISABILITIES

As in wheelchair basketball, volleyball can be adapted so that athletes with a physical disability can still participate – often at levels of skill and agility higher than many able-bodied players in the standard game! However, whilst a version of wheelchair volleyball is possible, the fact that volleyball is essentially a game of passing, rather than one where players can hold possession, means that non-wheelchair versions have been more successful.

Standing volleyball has its origins in Great Britain after the Second World War, arising out of the rehabilitation philosophy of 'Sport as Therapy' introduced by Sir Ludwig Guttmann at Stoke Mandeville Hospital for people with amputations. It is played in exactly the same way as the standard game but a points system for the varying degrees of disability is applied, to ensure that teams are evenly matched in terms of the overall disability levels. Standing volleyball entered the Paralympics in 1976 and is currently played at the international level by men only.

Sitting volleyball has a shorter history, dating back to 1953 and to a German game called Sitzball for athletes with lower-limb disability or amputation. The game was found to be too static and in 1956 a combination of Sitzball and volleyball was introduced in Holland. Sitting volleyball was introduced into the Paralympics in 1980 and found its way to Britain in

1984. One big advantage of sitting volleyball is that it can be played both by disabled athletes and the able-bodied. Unlike the standing game, sitting volleyball is also played at the international level by women.

groupings ensure that competing teams have roughly the same total level of disability on court at any one time.

For standing volleyball there is an extra official at the scorer's table whose job it is to check, at the start of each set and whenever a substitution is made, that the team total is above the minimum disability total required under the competition rules.

● STANDING VOLLEYBALL

The only difference between standing volleyball and the standard indoor game is the classification system. This assigns to each player an agreed category of disability, and these broad

Sitting volleyball. A lower net and a smaller court, but just as strenuous – and just as exciting! Players must generally remain in contact with the floor – the exception being for extreme recovery shots – otherwise the fault of lifting occurs.

● SITTING VOLLEYBALL

The major differences in sitting volleyball are modifications to the playing facility, and those which arise from the requirement that players must normally maintain contact with the floor.

The playing court for the sitting game measures 10m × 6m (instead of 18m × 9m); the net height is 1.15m for men, and 1.05m for women (instead of 2.43m and 2.24m). These two factors – the smaller court and the lower net – have the effect of making sitting volleyball appear much faster than the standard indoor game.

The attack line is placed 2m rather than 3m from the net. The rule relating to the centre line is also slightly different. Feet are permitted to cross this line under the net completely, providing there is no interference with the opponents.

Sitting volleyball has exactly the same restrictions on the positions of the players, at the moment of service. However, a player's position is determined by the position of the buttocks, rather than the position of the feet. (This means, for example, that a server can have feet 'on court' at the moment of service – providing that the buttocks remain behind the end line.)

To limit the effectiveness of the served ball, it is permitted in sitting volleyball for front-row players to block or attack the service.

In sitting volleyball some part of the body between the buttocks and the shoulders must normally be in contact with the floor; a player can contact the ball whilst rolling backwards, for example. If a player is not in such contact with the floor when playing the ball, this constitutes the fault called **lifting.** Players may not get up and move across the court, and then sit down to play the ball. The exception to this rule is an **extreme recovery** shot, when a player dives to save a ball – in this situation alone, a player may leave the floor for a *short* time.

RULE TRENDS

Volleyball is over one hundred years old. Unlike those sports which came into being over a period of time volleyball was devised, by William G. Morgan, in 1895, and followed the introduction of basketball, just three years earlier. Both sports were responses from educationalists to the need for non-violent games where skill and team spirit could be more important than sheer strength. Between 1895 and 1947 volleyball spread from the United States, largely via the YMCA movement. Although a relatively young sport, its rules were not always officially codified and it was often possible to modify the rules according to the age, sex, number and ability of the players involved. Originally the game consisted of nine innings (as in baseball) and players were allowed to dribble the ball (as in basketball). Volleyball was designed to incorporate the characteristics of two other sports – tennis and handball – and those purists who resist each

additional rule change should remember that it is the natural way of things for the rules of any sport to evolve over time. This reflects changes in physical factors – such as the height and agility of players, the construction and design of equipment and so on – and also the socio-economic environment, including the demands made by television and the need to retain the nature of the game as a spectacle.

In 1947 the formation of the FIVB led to a greater unification of the official rules and the imposition on each affiliated country of a standard way to play the game. The rules have subsequently undergone many further changes, aimed at meeting the basic requirements for a modern spectator sport.

Between 1947 and 1963 the main thrust of rules development was aimed at giving players more freedom to play the ball; additional flexibility was given to service reception by making it possible for a back-court player to move to the net and act as the main setter for the next attack. By 1951 the server was permitted to stand any distance away from the court and to run or jump before serving; the introduction of the attack-line in 1949 gave back-court players the right to hit the ball over the net, providing they took off from the back zone of court. Other changes during this period included the raising of the minimum ceiling height to 7m, the prohibition on screening the service and the limitation to six substitutions per team.

The period 1964 to 1979 saw volleyball's rise as a major Olympic sport; rules were changed during this time with a view to improving the impact of volleyball for spectators. The main purpose has been to preserve the balance between attack and defence; when the attack becomes too strong there is no opportunity for spectacular field defence, as the rallies are too short. To restrict the attack, the net crossing space was limited in 1972 by the introduction of two flexible rods, placed 9.40m apart on the top of the net; in 1976 these antenna were moved even closer together (to 9m) in order to reduce the power of the attack still further. To give an advantage to defending blockers, players were permitted in 1964 to make a second touch after the block and in 1972 to encroach into the opponents' court, providing their feet remained at least partly over the centre line. A major change in 1976 permitted a team to have three further touches after a block, thus removing the block altogether from a team's permitted number of contacts.

Since 1980 the influence of television and the demands of public entertainment and sponsorship potential have continued to exert pressure on the game's rule-makers. The need to have shorter matches – or, at least, matches of more predictable duration – has led to the modification of the scoring system. A point limit was introduced in 1988, to prevent sets going beyond 17 points. (This requirement was abandoned, for the final set only, in 1992.) At the same time the idea of rally point, where even the non-serving team can score a point, was introduced into the deciding set. The use of the three-ball system (from 1974) was designed to speed up the game by reducing the number of unnecessary stoppages and dead-ball time, as was the introduction in 1988 of the referee's delay sanctions to prevent, amongst other things, excessive sweat-wiping, shoelace-tying and other attempts at trying to slow the game down!

To improve a defender's chance when receiving a service or hard-hit attack, the ball pressure was reduced in 1980 and it seems likely that this will be reduced still further. In 1984 a defender was permitted to make a double touch when taking the first ball, and this was further extended to include playing the ball with a volley in

1994. Blocking service was banned altogether in 1984 and in 1994 players were given permission to serve from anywhere across the whole end line.

The third major trend in recent rule changes – boosting the attractiveness for spectators – has involved trying to eliminate minor technical faults, where these do not interfere with play, and looking at the needs of television, when covering major events. In the former category comes allowing players to make slight, unintentional contact with the net and permitting the ball to touch the legs (1992) and feet (1994); in the latter category comes the possibility of having a technical time-out or a service delay (in order to allow for action replays) and the 'wiring-up' of the first referee, to provide explanations of decisions over the public-address system!

The most recent rule changes – ratified at the 1996 Olympic Congress in Atlanta – include allowing hands to go over the centre line, a reduction in ball pressure, permitting the ball to be retrieved from outside the antennae and changes to the awarding of the misconduct warning (yellow card).

Teachers should understand how, and why, the rules of a game evolve; readers should also be aware that the International Rules are changed mostly with top-level volleyball in mind. The basic rules give volleyball its unique character and also permit numerous variations – for children and adults, for men and women, as a leisure activity or a top professional sport, for athletes with disability and for either six-a-side indoors or for two-a-side on sand.

MATCH PROTOCOL

The precise match protocol, i.e. the way any particular game of volleyball is presented to the public, is not covered within the official rules; rather, this is left to the individual organizers of any competition. However, there are general guidelines which dictate how the pre-match protocol is arranged, and one possible playing protocol is given below.

(a) 17 minutes before the start
Referees make a final check on the height and tension of the net and also check the antennae and side bands.

(b) 16 minutes before start
Captains report to scorer's table, to make the toss. Once the toss is taken, the captains should sign the scoresheet.

(c) 15 minutes before start
Start of official warm-up at the net; five minutes for each team separately, or 10 minutes together.

(d) 5 minutes before start
End of warm-up. Players go to the team benches to prepare. Coaches present the starting line-up sheets to the scorer.

(e) 3 minutes before start
Presentation of players and referees to the crowd; teams line up on court.

(f) 2½ minutes before start
Players shake hands at the net and prepare to start the match.

(g) 1 minute before start
First referee whistles for starting players to go on court; second referee checks court positions and indicates that match can begin.

In matches where there is to be no presentation of players, this protocol is adapted so that (c) and (d) start three minutes later and (e) and (f) are omitted altogether.

TERMINOLOGY

aerials   See **antennae.**

aggression   An actual or intended physical attack, for which the sanction is **disqualification.** (Not to be confused with 'aggression through the net', the popular term for the much lesser offence of intimidating opponents.)

antennae   The two flexible rods fastened 9m apart, at each end of the net, which mark out the **crossing space** on top of the net. Also called **aerials.**

assisted hit   When a player takes support from a team-mate or some other object, in the playing area, in order to reach the ball.

attack-hit   Any action which directs the ball towards the opponent (except service and block).

attack-line   The line drawn 3m away from, and parallel to, the centre line, on each side of the court; this line restricts the area from which back-court players can make attack-hits.

back zone   The 6m × 9m region behind the attack line; sometimes called **back court**.

back-court attack   An attack-hit carried out by a **back-row player.**

back-row player   A player currently playing in back-court positions 1, 6 or 5.

ball 'in'   The ball is 'in' when any part of it touches the court or boundary lines.

ball 'in play'   The ball is 'in play' from the moment of service hit.

ball 'out'   The ball is 'out' when it is not 'in'!

ball 'out of play'   The ball is 'out of play' when a fault is committed, or when one of the referees blows the whistle.

ball retrievers   The people (usually six) who fetch and feed the ball to the servers when a **three-ball system** is used.

base line   See **end line**.

blocking   The action of players who are close to the net, who reach above the top of the net in an attempt to intercept a ball which has been directed by opponents towards the net.

block attempt   The action of blocking without actually touching the ball.

boundary lines   Lines around the court, i.e. the **end lines** and the **side lines**.

carry   Also 'carried ball'. See **held ball**.

centre line   The line under the net which divides the court into two halves.

change of courts   When teams change ends in between sets, or at eight points in the final set.

completed attack   An attack-hit is completed when it completely crosses the plane of the net or is blocked.

completed block   The action of blocking when the ball is actually touched by a blocker.

collective block   When two or three players standing close to each other make a blocking action at the net.

collective screen   When the server is hidden behind a group of two or more team-mates and the ball is served over them.

crossing space   The part of the vertical plane of the net over which the ball must cross during play, i.e. the region over the top of the net and between the antennae.

default   When a team refuses to play, or when it does not appear on court by the agreed time, it is declared in default and **forfeits** the match.

delay   Any action which slows the game down unnecessarily.

delay warning   A yellow card given against the team, for the first delay in a set.

delay penalty   A red card given against the team, for the second and subsequent delays.

dig   The action of playing the ball below waist height, with the arms.

disqualification   When a player is sent off for the remainder of the match.

double contact   When a player contacts the ball twice in succession or the ball contacts more than one part of the body at different times; this is illegal except when blocking and on the first team contact. Also called **double touch**.

double fault   When opponents commit a fault at exactly the same time. After a double fault, the rally is replayed. Also called a 'replay' or a 'playover'.

double touch   See **double contact**.

end line   The 9m line at each end of the court. Also called the **base line**.

exceptional substitution   If an injured player cannot be legally substituted, an exceptional substitution (i.e. one which is otherwise considered illegal) is then allowed.

expulsion   When a player is sent off for the remainder of the set in progress.

fault   Any playing action contrary to the rules, resulting in the loss of a rally.

first referee   The official in overall control of the match.

first team contact   Whenever a player is making the first of a team's three permitted touches of the ball, excluding the block. This is not just when receiving service but any time when the ball comes over the net from the opponents.

forfeit   See **default.**

four contacts   See **four hits.**

four hits   The fault committed if a team uses more than its three permitted contacts in order to return the ball. Also called **four contacts** or **four touches.**

free zone   The symmetrical area around the outside of the playing court; this area must be free from any obstruction and should be a minimum of 3m wide.

front-row player   A player currently playing in front-court positions 2, 3 or 4.

front zone   The 3m × 9m area in front of the **attack line**. Also called the **front court.**

game captain   The captain on court; normally the same as the **team captain.**

game interruptions   Divided into the **regular** interruptions (**time-outs** and **substitutions**) and the **exceptional** interruptions (injury, external interference).

held ball   When a player does not hit the ball cleanly, and the ball rests momentarily in the hands. Also called a **carry**, a lift or a push.

incomplete team   A team which is reduced to five players is declared **incomplete** and loses the set (or the match).

illegal block   A block containing a back-row player, in which the ball is contacted.

illegal substitution   A substitution not permitted under the rules.

improper request   A request for interruption (time-out or substitution) which is made at the wrong time, or by the wrong person, or when a team has already had the maximum number permitted.

individual screen   When a single player waves arms, jumps or moves sideways at the moment of service and the ball is served over this player.

interruptions   See **game interruptions.**

interval   The period of three minutes between sets.

invasion   Popular term for **reaching** over the net.

line judge   One of four (or possibly just two) officials whose main task is to judge whether the ball has landed 'in' or 'out'.

line-up sheet   The list of players, in service order, who will begin the set. Also called a **rotation slip.**

misconduct   Incorrect conduct by an individual team member.

misconduct warning   A yellow card awarded for **unsportsmanlike conduct.**

misconduct penalty   A red card awarded for **rude conduct.**

net fault   When a player touches the net, or when the ball touches the net on service.

net height   2.43m (men) and 2.24m (women), measured at the centre of the net.

offensive conduct   Defined in the rules as 'defamatory or insulting words or gestures' and sanctioned by **disqualification**.

official warm-up   See **warm-up session**.

penalty   The 'red card'. See **delay penalty** and **misconduct penalty**.

penetration   The act of moving under the net into the opponents' court. Also refers to a tactical system of play in which a player moves from back court into front court in order to set up the attack.

playing area   The area which includes the **playing court** and the **free zone.**

playing court   The 18m × 9m rectangle on which the ball must land to be 'in'.

playing fault   See **fault**.

playing surface   Must be flat, horizontal and uniform, made of wood or synthetic material.

point limit   The system of scoring in the first four sets, where once the score reaches 16–16, the first team to reach 17 points wins the set.

positions   The regions on court occupied by front-court players 2 (right), 3 (centre) and 4 (left) and by back-court players 1 (right), 6 (centre) and 5 (left).

positional fault   When players are not in their correct positions at the moment of service.

protest   When the explanation of the referee does not satisfy a captain, a protest can be made at the end of the game, in writing and on the scoresheet.

rally   The period between the moment of the service hit until play is stopped by a referee's whistle or a fault being committed.

rally point   The system of scoring in the final set, where every rally results in a point being scored, irrespective of which team served. Also called **tie-break**.

reaching   The fault committed when a **blocker** places hands completely over the top of the net and makes contact with the ball, before the opponents have completed an attack-hit. (Popularly called 'invasion'.)

red card   The card used to indicate a **penalty**.

rotation   When a team regains the service, its players must rotate one position clockwise (player in position 2 rotates to position 1 to serve, player in 1 rotates to 6, and so on).

rotation fault   When the wrong player serves.

rotation order   The order in which players serve. See **service order**.

rotation slip   Another name for the **line-up sheet**.

rude conduct   Misconduct defined as 'acting contrary to good manners or moral principles, or expressing contempt'; sanctioned by the red card.

scorer Official responsible for filling in the scoresheet and keeping score.

screening The action of preventing opponents from seeing the server and the path of the served ball.

second referee The assistant to the first referee, occasionally referred to as the 'umpire'.

service The act of putting the ball into play by the right back-row player, who hits the ball with one hand or arm.

service attempt When the ball, having been tossed in the air or released, lands without touching the server, it is a service attempt.

service authorization When the referee whistles and signals to permit the service.

service order See **rotation order**.

set The period of play which ends when one team reaches 15 points, providing it has a two-point lead. See also **point limit**.

set interval See **interval**.

service zone The 9m-wide area behind each end line, from which players must serve. This zone extends as far back as the free zone allows.

side bands Two white bands, 5cm wide and 1m long, at each end of the net and 9m apart.

side line The 18m line down each side of the court.

side out Popular term for when the serving team loses service.

simultaneous contact When the ball is contacted by two players at exactly the same time.

smash See **spike**.

spike A powerfully hit shot with the open hand, directed towards the opponents' court. Also called the **smash.**

starting line-up The list of the six players who will start the set. See **line-up sheet**.

states of play See **ball in play** and **ball out of play**.

substitute A player not in play, i.e. not on court but sitting on the bench.

substitution The act of changing one player for another.

substitution zone The area off-court in front of the scorer's table, between the attack lines, where substitutions must take place.

successive contact When the ball is contacted twice, one followed by another.

team bench Located beside the scorer's table, in the **free zone**. The coach and the substitutes must sit here when they are not in the warm-up zone.

team captain The player who represents the team at the toss and signs the scoresheet.

team hits To return the ball over the net, a maximum of three hits (excluding any contacts with the block) is allowed.

temperature The minimum temperature is normally 10°C. For international matches the allowed temperature range is 16°C to 25°C.

three-ball system   For major events, three balls are used instead of only one. See **ball retrievers**.

tie-break   See **rally point**.

time-out   A pause of 30 seconds during the set, requested by either team, for the purpose of allowing the coach to speak with the players.

toss   Before the match begins, a coin is tossed and the captains choose who will serve first and at which ends the teams will play.

unsportsmanlike conduct   Misconduct of a minor nature, sanctioned by the yellow card.

volley   The basic skill of passing the ball, using open hands and making contact using the fingers only.

warm-up   General stretching and practising exercises before a game. See also **official warm-up**.

warm-up areas   Areas outside the free zone, in the bench-side corners, where players can warm-up whilst waiting to go on court.

warm-up session   A period of five minutes per team (often taken as ten minutes together) immediately before the match begins, in which players are permitted to use the net. Also called **official warm-up**.

warning   The yellow card; see also **delay warning** and **misconduct warning**.

yellow card   The card used to indicate a **warning**.

INDEX

Page numbers in **bold** refer to the illustrations